Trio Tapestry
Piano Accompaniment
by Joanne Martin

Contents

Alfred Music
P.O. Box 10003
Van Nuys, CA 91410-0003
alfred.com

Copyright © 2004 Summy-Birchard
a division of Summy-Birchard
exclusively distributed by Alfred Music
All Rights Reserved.

No part of this book shall be reproduced, arranged, adapted, recorded, publicly performed, stored in a retrieval system,
or transmitted by any means without written permission from the publisher. In order to comply with copyright laws, please apply for
such written permission and/or license by contacting the publisher at alfred.com/permissions.

ISBN-10: 1-58951-176-X
ISBN-13: 978-1-58951-176-7

Instrument photos courtesy of The Potter Violin Company and
Paesold Stringed Instruments, USA
Contact Jason Torreano
(800) 426-7068, Ext. 411
www.Paesold.com

ROCKING CHAIR

JOANNE MARTIN

ROBOT RODEO

JOANNE MARTIN

PIZZICATO

JOANNE MARTIN

TEASING

JOANNE MARTIN

ORIENTALE

JOANNE MARTIN

VALSE PARISIENNE

JOANNE MARTIN

GREENVILLE BLUES

JOANNE MARTIN

AUTUMN WALTZ

JOANNE MARTIN

THREE-LEGGED MARCH

JOANNE MARTIN

BERCEUSE

JOANNE MARTIN

CALYPSO

JOANNE MARTIN

PAINT RAG

JOANNE MARTIN

BLUE WALTZ

JOANNE MARTIN

JANUARY TANGO

JOANNE MARTIN